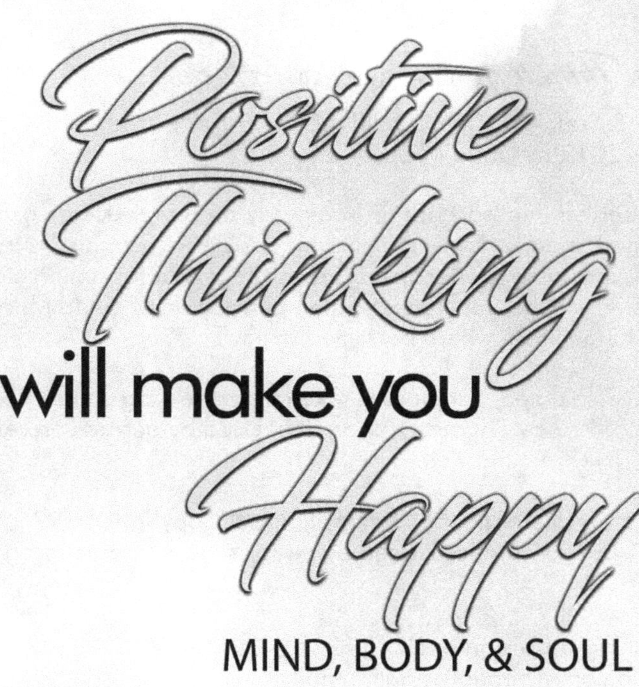

MIND, BODY, & SOUL

— 40-DAY JOURNAL —

LINDA M. JOHNSON

Positive Thinking will make you *Happy*

Mind, Body & Soul - 40-DAY JOURNAL

HOV Publishing a division of HOV, LLC.
www.hovpub.com / hopeofvision@gmail.com

Cover Design: HOV Design Solutions
Editor: Caroline Barnhill for Oak & State Communication

Write the author Linda M. Johnson at:
info@positivethinkingwillmakeyouhappy.com

For more information about special discounts for bulk purchases, please contact Linda M. Johnson or hopeofvision@gmail.com

Paperback ISBN: 978-1-942871-68-2
eBook ISBN: 978-1-942871-69-9
Library of Congress Control Number:

10 9 8 7 6 5 4 3 2

Printed in the United States of America

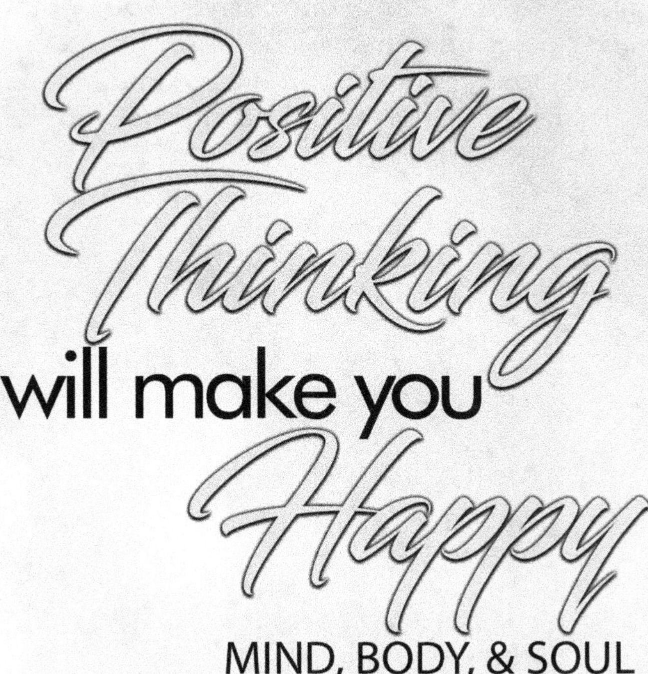
Positive
Thinking
will make you
Happy
MIND, BODY, & SOUL

Dedication

This book is dedicated to my nephew Chase McKee. You are greatly missed by your family and friends. Your Mommy Tina McKee sends kisses up to heaven because she knows you are sending kisses, too. I honor your memory, and the memory of all of the victims who perished on the day that you were born: 9/11.

In Loving Memory of Chase McKee
9/11/01 - 3/5/17

Endorsements

Linda Marshae Johnson writings are timely and essential for all who yearn for daily happiness amidst a successful career and life journey. Positive Thinking Will Make You Happy – Mind, Body and Soul is a powerful book about the irrepressible truth of the existential value of faith, and how what we think about contributes profoundly to one's state of happiness, joy and self-affirmation. I highly recommend this book for all people of all faiths who affirm the oneness of humanity.

~ Dr. Benjamin F. Chavis, Jr.
President and CEO, National Newspaper Publishers Association (NNPA)

"Windsong Wilkins (Linda Johnson) has been my dear sister and friend since High school. Her life is defined by her faith, her positive attitude and her determination to be her best self and to assist others in achieving their best in life. Her book, "Positive Thinking Will Make You Happy - Mind, Body & Soul" , will bless your life and uplift your spirit.

~ Bishop Darren A. Ferguson
Father, Husband, Pastor - Theophilus

Positive Thinking is how I live my life each day. I can personally attest to the great benefits of it. For as long as I've known Linda Johnson, she's always been a positive thinker. I have seen how it has made her life jubilant and more fulfilled. This book is a testament on how to follow her application.

~ Michele Leone Williams
NBC Today Producer

Special Messages to the Author

To one of my dearest and closest friends, Linda Marshae' Johnson. You have been an inspiration and support to so many. I've watched you over the years believe in, love on and carry so many. Your tenacity and drive have been a guiding light in such a dark world at times. You're my sister, confidante and true friend. When you set out on a task, you fight to the bitter end to achieve it. When all hell breaks loose, you still are unwavering. You are extremely trustworthy in all you do. You're a rare breed in that your word is your word. I have the honor and privilege to call you sister and friend for over 20 years. Never lose who you are, though you fight many battles. Your strength has given strength to others - especially me. I love you and never give up. Keep getting up for the fight is already won.
~ Monique Lisa

We love all of the stories you read to us, especially the ones you make up. We especially love the songs that you write and teach us how to sing them all using your rhythm and drill method. We love you Ya-Ya. Congratulations on your book.
~ Your grandchildren

We believe in you Mama Deuce. We know it has not been easy for you and Dad, but you hung in there and pursued your passions. You make us all so proud of you.
~ Your step-Children

Conversations with Linda Johnson are always inspiring, fascinating, and unique. Expect that and more from this book from such a charming and strong Woman of God.
~ Evangelist Sharon Henderson

Keep that positive thinking up
Keep that positive praying up
Keep those positive feelings up
Keep that positive smile on your face
Keep that positive voice strong
Keep that powerful magnetic energy all the way up to the sky
Keep that positive and consistency in motion and in order
Come on Linda Johnson, you are a Powerhouse all by yourself
~ Skyy Power10

I want to first thank my Father God for allowing me to be here to write this.

Secondly, I want to thank you Linda for giving me this platform to send positive words of encouragement to other people. I thought that using the acronym HOPE would be befitting.

H | I knew that God was preparing to **H**eal my body.
O | I was always **O**ptimistic about my healing.
P | I **P**raised and **P**rayed to my Father God through the hard times.
E | **E**arly detection is the key.

~ Lena Johnson

I thank God for my Best Friend Linda Marshae' Johnson who has been in my life since the age of 12. By the grace of God, we have never left one another's side - no matter the distance between us. Linda and I have shared very dark, deep valley experiences that we have been through and somehow God has blessed her with the ability to make such a powerful impact in the lives of others by telling these stories. There is nothing greater than having a best friend who believes in and knows the power of prayer. I am so proud of Linda and applaud her today. I truly admire the way that she has endured and stayed the course. It has encouraged me, and many others I am sure. I am grateful to God to have you in my life. To God be all the Glory.

In the Love and Luxury of Jesus,
~ Vivian Yvette Richburg

I was amazed at your ability to sing when we first met in our music class at John F. Kennedy High School. But I am even more amazed at your ability to write a story. As you grace the storytelling industry with your written works, I pray that lives will be touched in a positive way, souls will be won for the Kingdom of God, and millions of your books will be sold all over the world.
~Your friend for Life, Bob Arrington

Linda is a true example of what living by faith is all about. She has always remained positive through every battle I have watched her face. I have read many of her stories and strongly believe that every one of them is life-changing and inspirational.
~Sheila Cooper

I am so thankful that Linda Johnson asked me to read some of her manuscripts and give my input. She is a fascinating writer and remains a pillar of strength for everyone who knows her story. I strongly believe that she will be one of the greatest inspirational storytellers of all time.
~ Angela Cooper

There is only one word that expresses our friendship and her ability to tell a story – POWERFUL!
~ Adrienne Whaley a.k.a. Baby

I am so thankful to have met you and was even more blessed to coordinate you and Thomas's wedding. I have witnessed the many challenges you have faced and am so thankful that

you never gave up on pursuing your dreams. You are a real dream achiever.
~ Your friend, Aisha Willis

There is nothing too hard for God. Daughter-in-law, we believe that you will inspire many through your passion to write a powerful story. Keep God first in all you do and continue to remain faithful to Him. We encourage you to keep the flame of passion burning bright.
~ Pastor Thomas & Sis. Lani Johnson

I have been afforded the opportunity to write with Linda on various writing projects. Keep up the amazing work Linda.
~ Charlie Irvin

When I think about mind, body & soul, I see how one can't function without the other. I see Linda in this same way. I remember asking her about being in the Awesome Women On The Move INSPIRATIONAL Daily Journal book and how her mind was made up instantly. We know her body was afflicted, but she still came out to support the movement. Despite everything, her soul kept striving to be that awesome woman on the move.
~ Tenaria Drummond-Smith
Founder/Visionary of Awesome Women On The Move

The day I met Linda; I knew that she was destined for greatness. She is a true overcomer! She is truly one of my best friends ever since junior high school at John Peter Tetard - Class of 1984. Linda, my friend...the best is yet to come!
~ Donald B. Williams.

Linda has helped many artists to pursue their singing careers, help so many actors/actresses to get a role in stage plays and

commercials, and also helped me during a difficult time in my life. She deserves all of God's goodness because no matter the pain she has suffered for many, many years, she will not quit. She never gave up on her dreams, especially her passion of storytelling.
~ Michelle Barbara Hutcherson

We are so excited for Linda because she has worked so hard down through the years as an executive assistant sitting behind a desk for major corporations, and no one has ever known the jewel that was hidden in the treasure in her ability to tell a story. Linda writes from a true place of passion that captivates, mesmerizes and energizes everyone who has read her stories. I look forward to Linda M. Johnson making a great name in the industry as one of the bestselling successful creative writers and a great storyteller.
~ Mary Jones

It was a real pleasure having you as an MFA creative writer at the College of New Rochelle. The Langston Hughes House was a great place to write many of your amazing stories that are guaranteed to stir up the gift that is in you to bless the entire universe. Thank you for inspiring us with your stories.
~ The Library Staff at CNR

Keep your mind focused on Jesus and let him use you as an empty vessel to tell your stories to His glory. I believe that anything you put your mind to, Linda Bird, will bring you great success and much prosperity. Just remain positive, and you can do it!
~ Love your Grandfather, Richard Johnson

Big Sis. I applaud you for never giving up even through sickness and disease, the economic crisis, Hurricane Sandy that almost took your life, and every other obstacle that tried to stop you

from pursuing your passion to publish your books. You never gave up or quit! For this, Linda Bird, I celebrate you for doing what God has instructed you to do: sharing your testimonies and telling your stories of truth with passion.
~ Hope Johnson

Lil Sis keep on writing as God avails your mind, body and soul to write according to his will the things He leads you to put down on the pages. I believe in your ability to tell the most amazing stories.
~ Terrie Holmes

Keep up the good work Lil Sis. I always knew that one day you would pursue all of your dreams and aspirations. You are a real role model for our family to follow. I hope that you will make writing your full-time job because you are really good. I love you Linda Bird and am cheering for you, so keep up the good work.
~ Cleveland Johnson

Linda Bird, I always knew that you would write a book one day because you loved telling your stories. You are a real inspiration to our family, and I know that your Aunt Carrie is smiling down from heaven on you. Thank you for always being an overachiever and pursuing your dreams and aspirations despite all of the odds that sickness and disease may have caused you. I'm looking to see you on the BIG screen next!
~ Uncle Willie Murray

Congratulations on all of your accomplishments Sis. a.k.a. Windsong Wilkins. We love and thank God for you.
~ Bryan, Tara and Tyra

Ujamaa Black Theater would like to congratulate Linda Johnson for being a pioneer of a company for 30 years and counting. Linda's drive for performing arts has set the blueprint for all those artists who have come after her. Linda Johnson has encouraged the legacy of the theater with current Director Tajmal Walker after the passing of the founder, Titus Walker in 2009. Her motto in life has always been and still remains, 'Positive Thinking Will Make You Happy.'
~ Director Tajmal Walker and The Ujamaa Black Theater

Dear daughter – thank you for never giving up on your dreams no matter how hard it seemed. We are very proud of you.
~ Love Your Father, Tyrone & Sandra Wilkins

Linda, you make me so proud to be your husband. I am so glad that even after thirty plus years, you never gave up on the vision that God gave you for 'Positive Thinking Will Make You Happy' – you confessed it, believed in it, lived it, prayed it, sung it and walked in it every day. Today, it has finally manifested and will soon speak for itself – it will be seen all over the world on billboards, moving vehicles and seen on all of the products that God has placed in your heart to share this inspirational message to the world. I love and support you in all that you do, so keep on writing with passion baby! I love you with all of my heart and despite all of the odds that you and I have faced together; you always remained optimistic and held on to your faith in God. For this you deserve all of the goodness that is about to come your way. You are my queen for life.
~ Your husband, Minister Thomas W. Johnson, IV

Preface

Positive Thinking will make you Happy

This book, 40-Day Journal 'Positive Thinking Will Make You Happy' - Mind, Body and Soul, an inspirational book based on a real-life supernatural experience that changed author Linda Marshae' Johnson's life forever. She believes it can help readers to think positively in all aspects of their everyday life.

Linda testifies during her 40-Day journey about how the power of God brought her through life's difficulties despite the many setbacks and challenges she has faced over the past decade and a half. Linda emphasizes how a positive mindset and an optimistic outlook can get individuals through anything in life. Her 40-Day journey gives the reader true demonstrations of how having faith in God has sustained her; in spite of the many trials and tribulations she has faced as a career woman and the hardships that financial strain has impacted her life. She also reveals how the difficulties of living with Multiple Sclerosis (a debilitating medical condition) can cause unexpected circumstances. This has been a condition that she has suffered with for more than 30 years. However, her strong faith in God has delivered her through every challenge.

Linda's strong faith in God has given her wisdom, revelation and knowledge to empower others through a series of prayers, scriptures, affirmations and quotes. This daily practice has given her strength in maintaining a positive mindset, despite these adversities. This apparatus of sacrifice has given her victory over them all. These reflections of positive vibes allow her to enjoy the essence of God's presence.

Introduction

Personally, I feel that being positive makes you exceptional because of your mindset. You can't be positive and negative at the same time, because one will overpower the other and then it becomes an issue. So, I say choose the "Positive."

Being positive helps you to live a life of Faith in God. The Bible says, "Without faith, it is impossible to please God, for he who comes to God must believe that He is God, and a rewarder of those who diligently seek Him." (Hebrews 11:6 NIV) God always intended for us to live our lives positively, absolutely depending on His Divine Plan for us. Being positive helps you to respect others, regardless of their negative behavior or attitude. We all have experienced many things in life. Linda has weathered the storms of life but yet she looks to the Creator for direction.

When you feel bad in your body, many times if we just put on that special dress or suit that brings out the best in us, it changes how we feel about ourselves and we can start our day on a positive note. As you walk down the street, you can say "Good Morning" and know that you have brightened up someone's day who may be hurting - physically, mentally, or emotionally. Always be kind to others with your positive attitude, it will make you feel so happy. Most of all, carry yourself in a respectful manner. This alone helps you to live a positive lifestyle. And always act the way you look and always say to others even if it's a bad day, "I'm well."

Review your own personal qualities and never compare yourself to anyone else or their situation. Yes, you've been hurt, but don't let it rule your heart. Let God always be in the driver's seat.

Don't even talk negative to yourself or others. This is a no, no all the time. If Mr. or Miss Negative says, "No you can't," you answer, "Yes I can because I can do all things through Christ which strengthens me." (Philippians 4:13) Always do what is good and comfortable to you. Never be a people pleaser, it will stir up the negative. Be the best you can be for God and present that to the world. Take charge of any negative thoughts that try to conquer your mind or upset your dreams. Uphold your happiness. Remember you are a positive thinker. Find ways to maintain your happiness, even if it's just reading a book or meditating on something beautiful you saw like a butterfly.

Lastly, a positive attitude is essential to happiness, joy, peace, and your development in life. This will make you very enthusiastic and give you a strong state of mind. Remember it's a mindset you possess and if you keep it positive, happiness will be yours for the asking. And even if something negative comes along, a positive mind will say everything is going to be alright because my faith is in Jesus Christ, my Savior who knows the thoughts He has towards me. Keep your mind strong and make sure you are getting enough rest and eating healthy. Believe God's word and write down the vision He shows you if you remain positive, He will make it plain to you. Separate yourself from family, friends, church members, or special acquaintances that don't have your best at heart. Stay Positive. Be Happy, don't allow anyone to tread on the place where only God dwells in your heart.

~ Evangelist Anne Gaynelle Johnson

Day 1

A Renewed Mind

God is love. His love cannot be compared to anything on this earth because it is eternal. A renewed mind will allow you to think positive. And a positive attitude will get you through every situation.

"Finally, brethren, whatsoever things are true, whatsoever things are honest, whatsoever things are just, whatsoever things are pure, whatsoever things are lovely, whatsoever things are of good report; if there be any virtue, and if there be any praise, think on these things." - Philippians 4:8

In order to have a renewed mind, you must ask yourself the question, "Am I ready to weed out the negative thoughts that the enemy, Satan, the father of lies, uses against me knowing it can cause me to spiral into a negative mindset of doubt and fear?

If you begin to experience the glory of God's goodness, become more aware of God's presence, and allow the Holy Spirit to make you aware every time He speaks to your heart, mind and soul, you are living in a constant awareness of God's presence. With this thought in mind, understand that the heart and the mind work hand-in-hand.

The peace of God that passes all understanding will begin to overtake you. God is the only one that can give you the everlasting peace of mind. Coming to a place in your walk with God as a believer, and entering into His presence, is one key component to having a renewed mind. God's peace will begin to fill your heart with an everlasting joy, even in the midst of a storm – whether that storm is grief, heartache, hurt, pain or suffering. Pray for peace; Let "The peace of God belongs to me," become your daily confession. Peace in your mind and in your thoughts.

"Thou wilt keep him in perfect peace, whose mind is stayed on thee: because he trusteth in thee." - Isaiah 26:3

Day 2

Do Not Worry

It takes faith to trust God at His word. It takes faith to believe that He will do the impossible. It takes faith to live a holy and righteous life that is pleasing to God. It takes faith to see things not as they seem, but trust that "It is already done!" It takes faith to praise God even when your body is tired and weary; things should look differently for those in Christ. It takes faith to move mountains. It takes faith to live a worry-free life.

Live your life to your fullest potential. For if you believe, you will receive whatever you ask God for in prayer. *"But seek ye first the kingdom of God, and his righteousness; and all these things shall be added unto you."* - Matthew 6:33

"Trust in the Lord with all your heart; and lean not unto thine own understanding. In all thy ways acknowledge him, and he shall direct your paths." - Proverbs 3:5-6

Day 3

God is Always with You

A test is a challenge, dear sisters and brothers of the Most High God. God will not give you more than you can bear, and He will never leave you, nor forsake you.

"My brethren, count it all joy when ye fall into divers temptations..." - James 1:2

"Blessed is the man that endureth temptation: for when he is tried, he shall receive the crown of life, which the Lord hath promised to them that love him." - James 1:12

"Be strong and of good courage, fear not, nor be afraid of them: for the LORD thy God, he it is that doth go with thee; he will not fail thee, nor forsake thee." - Deuteronomy 31:6

Day 4

Walk in The Spirit

Pray, daily, for a desire to walk in the power of the Spirit. In doing so, you will no longer want to fulfill the lust of your fleshly desires.

Lord, renew my mind daily. Lord, renew my heart daily. Lord, sanctify my soul daily. Dear God, impart unto me the goodness that comes from the fruits of the spirit. My body is the temple of the Holy Spirit. This is my daily prayer. *"Let this mind be in you, which was also in Christ Jesus."* - Philippians 2:5

"But the fruit of the spirit is love, joy, peace, longsuffering, gentleness, goodness, faith, meekness, temperance: against such, there is no law. And they that are Christ's have crucified the flesh with the affections and lusts. If we live in the Spirit, let us also walk in the Spirit." - Galatians 5:22-25

"I desire to be God's woman. A virtuous woman is hard to find." - Proverbs 31

Day 5

God's Divine Protection Over my Children

The love beyond my womb is my cry out to the Lord to save, sanctify, deliver and protect my children from all evil. For God has a purpose and a perfect plan for their lives. Father, I thank you for your divine protection, and I thank you for encamping my children surrounding them with your ministering angels and building a shield of protection keeping them in the ark of safety from all demonic forces.

Pause to pray Psalm 91 over your children.

He that dwelleth in the secret place of the Most High shall abide under the shadow of the Almighty.

I will say of the LORD, He is my refuge and my fortress: my God; in him will I trust. Surely he shall deliver thee from the snare of the fowler, and from the noisome pestilence.

He shall cover thee with his feathers, and under his wings shalt thou trust: his truth shall be thy shield and buckler.

Thou shalt not be afraid for the terror by night; nor for the arrow that flieth by day;

Nor for the pestilence that walketh in darkness; nor for the destruction that wasteth at noonday.

A thousand shall fall at thy side, and ten thousand at thy right hand; but it shall not come nigh thee.

Only with thine eyes shalt thou behold and see the reward of the wicked.

Because thou hast made the LORD, which is my refuge, even the most High, thy habitation;

There shall no evil befall thee, neither shall any plague come nigh thy dwelling.

For he shall give his angels charge over thee, to keep thee in all thy ways.

They shall bear thee up in their hands, lest thou dash thy foot against a stone.

Thou shalt tread upon the lion and adder: the young lion and the dragon shalt thou trample under feet.

Because he hath set his love upon me, therefore will I deliver him: I will set him on high, because he hath known my name.

He shall call upon me, and I will answer him: I will be with him in trouble; I will deliver him, and honour him.

With long life will I satisfy him, and shew him my salvation.

Day 6

Not to Know The Love of God

Not to know the love of God is a sad thing
Not to know the love of God is an aimless walk
Not to feel the love of God is a lonely place
Not to feel the indwelling of God's spirit is an empty vessel

Not to experience God's sovereignty is a loss benefit
Not to experience the unmerited favor of God is a wayward path
Not to hear God speak is a hopeless life of uncertainty
Not to hear the spirit of God Almighty is a dangerous pitfall

Not to receive wisdom and revelation from God is a cluttered mindset
Not to receive all that God has in store for you is an unfortunate feeling of loss
Not to live a prosperous and fruitful life full of joy, peace, mercy and grace is hopeless
Not to live in the fullness of God's holiness is a condemned soul

"For I know the thoughts that I think toward you, saith the LORD, thoughts of peace, and not of evil, to give you an expected end. Then shall ye call upon me, and ye shall go and pray unto me, and I will hearken unto you. And ye shall seek me, and find me, when ye shall search for me with all your heart." - Jeremiah 29:11-13

Day 7

A Place of Peace

The LORD JESUS CHRIST is the divine source of all true peace.

To be at peace in your mind, body and soul is to be at war with all else that will try to take God's place. To be at peace with God means to rest in Him and Him alone, not to depend on anything or anyone else. To be at peace with yourself is the place that is only obtainable through our Risen Lord and Savior Jesus Christ.

Pray this prayer for entering into a place of peace: *Dear Father, I am delighted that Jesus Christ, the God of Peace, is with me at all times. I give glory, honor and praise to Him. He is the perfection of all the godly qualities that reveals His character, strength and power that we read in the Scriptures passage which leads us to tranquility: He is noble, right, pristine, lovely, estimable, excellent and praiseworthy.*

Peace belongs to you always. The best thing you can do when you are filled with solicitousness and worry is to find a quiet place to pray, read your Bible, and heedfully hear to discern inspiriting worship and praise music that is soothing to your ears and enlightening to your mind.

God wants you to have a life. Living your life to the fullest, which includes being at peace. My prayer for you today is that the peace of God will overtake you like never before and that God's peace will be in your mind to calm your apprehensiveness and stress. Once you experience the peace of God and walk in it always, you are living a life that is guaranteed to give you true everlasting joy.

"Peace I leave with you, my peace I give unto you: not as the world giveth, give I unto you. Let not your heart be troubled, neither let it be afraid." - John 14:27

Day 8

You Left My Life So Expeditiously

Written By, Linda Marshae Johnson Aka (Windsong)

You Left My Life So Expeditiously
Just When I Was Getting To Know You
You Flew Away With The Angels In The Sky
Now All That I Can Ask Myself Is, "Why?"

Why Have I Lost You My Love?
I'd Give My Life For You My Dear
Never Ever Imagined You're Not Here
Wish That I Could Feel Your Presence So Near

You Left My Life So Expeditiously
I Didn't Even Get To Say Goodbye
New Life Just Seems So Mysterious
My Life With You Just Wasn't Meant To Be

You Left My Life So Expeditiously
Heaven Must Have Needed You My Love
I Try So Hard To Understand You See
Like A Flash In No Time You Were Gone

Forever You Will Be My One And Only Love
My Darling, Darling Baby You Are Forever With Me
Truly Devoted, Adored And All So Loved Forever
No One Could Ever Take Your Place, No Never
Only In My Dreams Is Where I See Your Face
I Feel Your Spirit And Your Warm Embrace
I Wish That I Could Have You Back Again
All To Myself And Rest In Your Wings

You Left My Life So Expeditiously
I Didn't Even Get To Say Goodbye
New Life Just Seems So Mysterious
My Life With You Just Wasn't Meant To Be

Day 9

...Like A Loose Garment - Let Go and Let God!

Wear This World Like A Loose Garment...
And You Will Not Be Devasted If It Should Suddenly Come To A Quick End.

Wear People Like A Loose Garment...
So You Will Not Be Hurt And Depressed If They Should Suddenly Walk Away Or Leave You.

Wear Material Possessions Like A Loose Garment...
So You Will Not Be Affected Or Caught Off Guard If They Are Suddenly Stripped Or Taken Away From You.

Wear Money And Wealth Like A Loose Garment...
For You Will Always Be Content In Life Regardless Of Your Financial Status.

Wear Your Relationship With God Like A Form-Fitted Garment...
And Hold On Very Tight To The Master's Hand.
For He Promised To Never Leave You Nor Forsake You. He Promised To Be With You Always, Even Until The Very End!

I don't know who this is for, but I am so glad I wrote it from my heart.

Day 10

Sometimes I Cry
(For The Sufferers Of Chronic Pain)

Over the past decade and a half, I have cried so many tears. Oftentimes, I have thought that God must have buckets of my tears in a store room in Heaven. I cry from the chronic pain that I live with daily. Many Christians may say that this is a negative thing to say about my condition. But, the truth of the matter is that this is my reality. It is not that I don't have faith, because I do believe that Jesus bore my pain on the cross, and with His stripes, I am healed, according to Isaiah 53:5. It states, "He was wounded for my transgressions, he was bruised for my iniquities, the chastisement of my peace was upon Him, and with His stripes I am healed." Honestly, I believe that with all of my heart, and still believe that my healing will manifest itself in the natural realm.

I wrote that passage 25 years ago.

Today I write....

Lord, I thank you for the pain that is a constant reminder that I am still alive.
Lord, I praise you that this pain will not stop me from living out my purpose.
Lord, I believe that this pain will never darken the flame of passion in my heart.
Lord, I'm so grateful that this pain cannot stop me from pursuing my dreams and aspirations.

P - Positive, Purpose, Plan
A - Ability, Actions, Able
I - Insight, Intelligence, Innovative
N - Newness, Necessary, Nurtured

Day 11

Positive Motivational Steps For Maintaining Success & Building Wealth

Here are some basic components for developing a positive mindset for maintaining success and building wealth:

- Breathing exercise: inhale through your nostrils & hold it; then exhale slowly pushing the air out of your mouth gently [repeat this three times] then let your body drop
- Breathing exercise: inhale through your mouth & hold it; then exhale slowly pushing the air out of your nostrils gently [repeat this three times] then let your body drop once again
- You are now preparing your body to enter into a state of tranquility, peacefulness and relaxation
- Relaxing peacefully to lessen the noise and allow the humility and compassion of Christ to embrace your mind
- Meditation – always find a quiet place where you can sit alone and be quiet before God and read your word
- Focus: New ambitions, divine purpose, dreams, aspirations and goals to achieve
- Determination: Ask for a positive determination to succeed in every aspect of your life
- Self-esteem: Accept yourself positively knowing that you are a child of the Most High God
- Patience: An overwhelming sense of comfort should overshadow your thoughts
- True to thyself: To thy own self, be true always in everything you do
- No doubt or anxiety can enter your mind at this point
- You will perform in excellence and be confident in your

work ethic

- Self-assuredness and confidence as a business professional will strengthen your earning potential
- Dignity, integrity, trustworthiness and reliability will become your new business minded characteristics
- You will begin to evaluate your life and reach decisions more effectively
- Let go of negative thinking: There will be a direct release of positive energy in your life
- Do nothing that will drain your emotions or resources
- Incorporate prayer and meditation as a way to think positive throughout your day
- Read positive affirmations along with your Bible (Consider the book of Psalms) and maintain positive confessions in all of your conversations
- I can, I will, I am, I shall, I believe…etc.: This will make you smile inside and outside
- No matter what you are going through, repetition of positive thoughts is the key to success
- Building wealth and power is another way to stay motivated and positive in your life
- Post positive things around you that you can see and say. Wealth starts with an optimistic attitude; God gives us power to get wealth (Deuteronomy 8:18)

    - I am, I believe, I can, I shall, etc.
    - Save your change.
    - Think B.I.G.
    - Have a plan for building wealth.

God's Favor

You are filled with favor and is esteemed by God because you are His child.

Self-esteem is just what it says, "self-esteem." To esteem oneself is to have self-respect and to have a favorable impression of oneself is the best way to describe self-esteem.

"I can do all things through Christ which strengtheneth me." - Philippians 4:13

"My soul, wait thou only upon God; for my expectation is from him. He only is my rock and my salvation: he is my defense; I shall not be moved." - Psalm 62:5-6

"For God hath not given us the spirit of fear; but of power, and of love, and of a sound mind." - 2 Timothy 1:7

Day 13

My Daily Devotion

When I first gave my heart to Jesus Christ and began to read the Holy Bible, I started from the very beginning in the book of Genesis not really understanding anything I was reading. But one day, I met a woman named Nancy who explained the importance of incorporating a specific time each day where I should go to pray and read my word. She also shared some basic scriptural references with me to get me started, and as I grew in the things of God, I built my own daily devotion that I would like to share with you. I hope that this will help you and build you up as you continue to grow stronger in the Lord each day.

My daily devotion starts with an unrehearsed silent prayer that I begin first by asking God for his forgiveness for all of my sins and my shortcomings. I then start thanking God for everything and everyone in my life, and as the Holy Spirit leads me based on what is happening in my family, church, job and the entire country, I pray over each of the areas. I always pray for leaders, my Pastor and his family, my church family and the body of Christ, our country and all of those who are in authority in this world. Praying that they will be surrounded by Godly men and women to help them to make wise and just decisions concerning our nation. I then praise God giving him all of the glory and honor that is due to him because He is a loving, kind, and merciful God who has given me life. Lastly, I remain silent after I pray and wait on the Lord. A few minutes later, I start reading the following scriptures and confessing them over myself making them personal for me. I am motivated and supercharged each day and I recommend you do the same as the Holy Spirit leads you.

Romans 10:8-10 – Sinner's Prayer for Salvation
Mark 11:23-25 and Hebrews 11:1,6 – Faith
Ephesians 1:17-19 – Spiritual Wisdom and Revelation Knowledge
Matthew Chapter 6 – Focuses on 3 major themes that are near and dear to my heart - The Kingdom of God; God's Providential Care; Spiritual Acts of Righteousness
Ephesians 3:20-21 – God is Able
Philippians 4:6-7 – Managing Anxiety
Proverbs 3:5-6 – Do Not Worry
Psalm 23 – God Our Protector and Provider
Psalm 100 – A Psalm of Praise
Ephesians 6:10-20 – 'Putting On The Whole Armor of God'
Psalm 91 - God's Divine Protection (the secret place)
God always protects His children in any and every situation. He will always be with us because He promises never to leave us nor forsake us. He is with us always. And He is with you always. You are protected and sheltered by the one true God who made heaven and earth.

"I am sheltered and protected in God." - Colossians 3:3

Day 14

I'm No Longer Living My Life on Eggshells

Living my life on eggshells
Coasting along the seashore
Giving each day a new start
Boasting daily, faithful hearts

I will walk and not faint at sudden calamity
Keeping my eyes on the One who watches over me
Doing what God commands for His glory
Giving Him praise and honor because He is holy

I am no longer living my life on eggshells
The Lord my God has loosened my shackles
No longer will the chains of sin keep me bound
My mind, my body and my soul are free from the state of stuck

Day 15

You Are An Overcomer

You are an overcomer by the blood of the lamb.

A positive attitude will get you through anything in life. It doesn't matter if it seems like you are losing, dying and the walls are crashing down on you. You must always stand firm on God's word, reading it daily and live a life that is driven by prayer as a born-again believer.

"And they overcame him by the blood of the Lamb, and by the word of their testimony; and they loved not their lives unto the death." - Revelation 12:11

"The LORD is my strength and my shield; my heart trusted in him, and I am helped: therefore my heart greatly rejoiceth; and with my song will I praise him." - Psalm 28:7

"For we walk by faith, not by sight." - 2 Corinthians 5:7

"The LORD is my light and my salvation; whom shall I fear? The LORD is the strength of my life; of whom shall I be afraid?" - Psalm 27:1

"Be careful for nothing; but in everything by prayer and supplication with thanksgiving let your requests be made known unto God. And the peace of God, which passeth all understanding, shall keep your hearts and minds through Christ Jesus." - Philippians 4:6-7

Day 16

God Has A Purpose and A Perfect Plan For Your Life

You are chosen for a divine purpose – it is the one that lasts because God fulfills His purpose for all of His children. Believe in yourself. You are destined for greatness! You are positively awesome!

Smile and be of good cheer because your life is in the Master's hand. He is the One who holds the sparrow... the One who stands right there beside you and me.

"Wherefore, my beloved, as ye have always obeyed, not as in my presence only, but now much more in my absence, work out your own salvation with fear and trembling. For it is God which worketh in you both to will and to do of his good pleasure."
- Philippians 2:12-13

Day 17

You Are No Longer A Slave To Sin

You are saved, set free and delivered from a life of sin. The Holy Bible says that we are, "Dead to Sin, Alive to God."

"What shall we say then? Shall we continue in sin, that grace may abound? God forbid. How shall we, that are dead to sin, live any longer therein? Know ye not, that so many of us as were baptized into Jesus Christ were baptized into his death? Therefore, we are buried with him by baptism into death: that like as Christ was raised up from the dead by the glory of the Father, even so we also should walk in newness of life. For if we have been planted together in the likeness of his death, we shall be also in the likeness of his resurrection: Knowing this, that our old man is crucified with him, that the body of sin might be destroyed, that henceforth we should not serve sin. For he that is dead is freed from sin.

Now if we have died with Christ, we believe that we shall also live with him: Knowing that Christ being raised from the dead dieth no more; death hath no more dominion over him. For in that he died, he died unto sin once: but in that he liveth, he liveth unto God. Likewise reckon ye also yourselves to be dead indeed unto sin, but alive unto God through Jesus Christ our Lord.

Let not sin therefore reign in your mortal body, that ye should obey it in the lusts thereof. Neither yield ye your members as instruments of unrighteousness unto sin: but yield yourselves unto God, as those that are alive from the dead, and your members as instruments of righteousness unto God. For sin shall not have dominion over you: for ye are not under the law, but under grace.

For all things are for your sakes, that the abundant grace might through the thanksgiving of many redound to the glory of God. For which cause we faint not; but though our outward man perish, yet the inward man is renewed day by day. For our light affliction, which is but for a moment, worketh for us a far more exceeding and eternal weight of glory; While we look not at the things which are seen, but at the things which are not seen: for the things which are seen are temporal; but the things which are not seen are eternal." - 2 Corinthians 4:14 -18

Day 18

There Is A Shift In The Atmosphere When You Pray

You are shifting the atmosphere because you have a prayer life.

Prayer is essential in the lives of believers, so don't ever stop communicating with God. Always include time to meditate on God's word after you pray. You must always leave room for God to speak to you.

Praying to God is an act of obedience and worship as it allows God to be in total control of our spirit. We must worship God in spirit and in truth according to His word, which calls us to pray.

"Confess your faults one to another, and pray one for another, that ye may be healed. The effectual fervent prayer of a righteous man availeth much." - James 5:16

"But ye shall receive power, after that the Holy Ghost is come upon you: and ye shall be witnesses unto me both in Jerusalem, and in all Judaea, and in Samaria, and unto the uttermost part of the earth." - Acts 1:8

Day 19

You Are Healed

You are healed from all of your diseases and afflictions.

"And he said unto her, Daughter, thy faith hath made thee whole; go in peace, and be whole of thy plague." - Mark 5:34

"And they said, if ye send away the ark of the god of Israel, send it not empty; but in any wise return him a trespass offering: then ye shall be healed, and it shall be known to you why his hand is not removed from you." - 1 Samuel 6:3

Always find a Scripture to stand on and confess, as often as you can, when you are faced with a health issue or medical challenge. One of my favorite Scriptures I stand on is Isaiah 53:5.

"Surely he hath borne our griefs, and carried our sorrows: yet we did esteem him stricken, smitten of God, and afflicted. But he was wounded for our transgressions, he was bruised for our iniquities: the chastisement of our peace was upon him; and with his stripes we are healed." - Isaiah 53:4-5

Day 20

God Has Called, Appointed and Anointed You

You have been called, appointed and anointed by God.

According to Romans 8:9, you are anointed of God, to be led by God.

"But the anointing which ye have received of him abideth in you, and ye need not that any man teach you: but as the same anointing teacheth you of all things, and is truth, and is no lie, and even as it hath taught you, ye shall abide in him." - 1 John 2:27

"Ye have not chosen me, but I have chosen you, and ordained you, that ye should go and bring forth fruit, and that your fruit should remain: that whatsoever ye shall ask of the father in my name, he may give it you." - John 15:16

Day 21

God Has Fully Equipped You To Do Anything You Put Your Mind To

In Romans 12:2, the apostle Paul urges that we should be transformed by the renewing of our minds to discern the will of God. The transformed mind can discern between the "wisdom of this age" and the "message of sapience among the mature." (1 Corinthians 2:6) The astute faculty that God has endowed man is far superior to that of any animal. The astute competency that God endowed man with is far beyond that of animals, and certainly that of which we see with our natural eyes. However, the things we see naturally are a reminder that we must renew our minds daily and walk in the spirit, asking God to help us to see through our spiritual eyes. In essence, this will increase our faith.

Pursuing your passion, which is what you were ultimately put on this earth to do, should be the number one thing that you are in pursuit of over and above anything else. You can do anything you put your mind to – especially when you have passion. God has placed certain gifts and talents in you in order to equip you to pursue your passion. Go for it because you are fully equipped and will begin to see positive results once you do it God's way. You can, and you will, succeed.

"I can do all things through Christ which strengthens me."
- Philippians 4:13

Day 22

Walk With An Attitude of High Expectations

You should live with high expectations from the Lord.

"For I know the thoughts that I think toward you, saith the Lord, thoughts of peace, and not of evil, to give you an expected end. Then shall you call upon me, and ye shall go and pray unto me, and I will hearken unto you. And ye shall seek me, and find me, when ye shall search for me with all your heart."
- Jeremiah 29:11-13

The word of God says, *"For my thoughts are not your thoughts, neither are your ways my ways, saith the LORD. For as the heavens are higher than the earth, so are my ways higher than your ways, and my thoughts than your thoughts."*
- Isaiah 55:8-9

Day 23

God Made You To Prosper

You are the head and not the tail; above and not beneath. You shall lend and not borrow. You are blessed beyond measure. You are sons and daughters of the King of Kings and the Lord of Lords. You come from a royal family so remember your royal position brothers, you are kings and sisters you are queens from a royal priesthood.

1 Peter 2:9 says, " But ye are a chosen generation, a royal priesthood, an holy nation, a peculiar people; that ye should shew forth the praises of him who hath called you out of darkness into his marvellous light;

Began to confess daily, "All my bills are paid and all of my needs are met," and watch things and negative conditions where your finances are concerned begin to change.

"This book of the law shall not depart out of thy mouth; but thou shalt meditate therein day and night, that thou mayest observe to do according to all that is written therein: for then thou shalt make thy way prosperous, and then thou shalt have good success." - Joshua 1:8

Day 24

You Are Fearfully and Wonderfully Made

You are fearfully and wonderfully made in God's image, so walk in that which He says you are.

"I will praise thee; for I am fearfully and wonderfully made: marvelous are thy works; and that my soul knoweth right well."
- Psalm 139:14

A Place of Peace

Entering into a place of peace is all that I longed for in my life. Throughout the course of my life, peace and tranquility were something that I realized was missing for far too long. I needed the peace of God in order to keep me from going insane. There is a song by a group called, the Pretenders, entitled, "Thin Line Between Love and Hate" that has become a known cliché, but is one that I strongly agree with. Moreover, I believe that there is also a thin line between a person being sane and insane. The point I am trying to make here is that we all have something on the inside of us that is either torturing us or causing us to gravitate toward something good or bad. Many people often admit that they are in a betwixt straight between the two. Now, some may agree, and some may not agree. However, the choice is truly up to each and every individual in this walk called, "life."

A place of peace calms the raging seas in our thoughts, our minds, our souls and our bodies. When Jesus said, "Peace be still," there was peace.

Day 25

God's Divine Protection Over My Grandchildren

The love beyond the seed of my womb is my cry out to the Lord to save, sanctify, deliver and protect my grandchildren from a life of sin. For God has a purpose and a perfect plan for their lives. Father, I thank you for your divine protection, and I thank you for encamping my grandchildren around and about with your ministering angels. Psalm 91

You also need to know God for yourself. Think about how God delivered you from that which once had you trapped and snared. You need to know the Holy Spirit is your comforter when you are sad, lonely, hurt or broken. You have to believe that God will forgive you of a sinful past because you are righteous and justified being in right standing with the Almighty God who loves you more than you will ever know. Jesus is a healer of all sickness, diseases, and bad habits. You should pray daily, asking the Holy Spirit to lead and guide you in this journey called life.

"That I may know him, and the power of his resurrection, and the fellowship of his sufferings, being made conformable unto his death; If by any means I might attain unto the resurrection of the dead. Not as though I had already attained, either were already perfect: but I follow after, if that I may apprehend that for which also I am apprehended of Christ Jesus. Brethren, I count not myself to have apprehended: but this one thing I do, forgetting those things which are behind, and reaching forth unto those things which are before, I press toward the mark for the prize of the high calling of God in Christ Jesus."

- Philippians 3:10-14

Day 26

A Positive Path For Holy and Righteous Living

God is holy and He requires you to be holy because you are His child. It takes faith and obedience to fulfill what He purposes for you to do in your heart and mind, in order to live according to the ordinances of a righteous God for a saved soul.

Therefore, with minds that are alert and fully sober, set your hope on the grace to be brought to you when Jesus Christ is revealed at his coming. As obedient children, do not conform to the evil desires you had when you lived in ignorance. But just as he who called you is holy, so be holy in all you do; for it is written: "Be holy, because I am holy." Since you call on a Father who judges each person's work impartially, live out your time as foreigners here in reverent fear. For you know that it was not with perishable things such as silver or gold that you were redeemed from the empty way of life handed down to you from your ancestors, but with the precious blood of Christ, a lamb without blemish or defect. He was chosen before the creation of the world, but was revealed in these last times for your sake. - 1 Peter 1:13-20 (NIV)

The Love of God

The love of God reaches higher than the highest mountain top
Far beyond the sky and space above it reaches everywhere
The love of God spreads throughout the lowest valley
The floor level beyond the abyss of the ocean's floor

The love of God is embedded in the core of my heart
The love of God is touching the myelin sheaths covering the nerves in my brain
The love of God is always on my mind from sun up to sun down
The love of God is always in my inner-most thoughts of peace beyond measure

The darkest waters of the deep blue sea
The misty fog fades my view of the clearing
The ocean is the shadow of the sky
The winds are whispering as the waves are whooshing by

Day 28

All That God Has Promised You

All that God has promised you claim it
All that God has promised you receive it
All that God has promised you love it
All that God has promised you enjoy it
All that God has promised you share it
All that God has promised you give it
All that God has promised you be thankful for it
All that God has promised you will manifest
All that God has promised you will come to pass
All that God has promised you believe it by faith
All that God has promised you is yours
All that God has promised you is an act of His kindness
All that God has promised you is just because you are His child
All that God has promised you is because He cares for you
All that God has promised you is because He loves you
All that God has promised you is because He wants the very best for you
All that God has promised you is because He spoke it into existence
All that God has promised you was predestined from the beginning
All that God has promised you is to give you His riches in glory
All that God has promised you is for you to have an abundant life
So always remember all that God has promised you

Day 29

Walk In Your Season

God is about to do His greatest work in your life. Yes, there have been many days and many nights of uncertainty, but God was always with you. He is always with you in the morning, noonday, evening and in the night of your darkest hour – when it seems that all hope is gone. God is always with you. He promised to never leave you, nor forsake you.

God has dispatched his ministering angels to have charge over your life. We must get to know Him, and love Him, more than anything or anyone else in this world. We must come to a place and a spiritual understanding in our walk with God where it is not just necessary, but extremely urgent, that we understand the importance of listening to God and knowing His voice. God still speaks today through His Word, other people, the preached Word, our situations and even audibly.

Day 30

Intimacy With God

God is right there waiting for you to give your heart to him.

(A Psalm of David, when he was in the wilderness of Judah.)

O God, thou art my God; early will I seek thee: my soul thirsteth for thee, my flesh longeth for thee in a dry and thirsty land, where no water is;

2 To see thy power and thy glory, so as I have seen thee in the sanctuary.

3 Because thy lovingkindness is better than life, my lips shall praise thee.

4 Thus will I bless thee while I live: I will lift up my hands in thy name.

5 My soul shall be satisfied as with marrow and fatness; and my mouth shall praise thee with joyful lips:

6 When I remember thee upon my bed, and meditate on thee in the night watches.

7 Because thou hast been my help, therefore in the shadow of thy wings will I rejoice.

8 My soul followeth hard after thee: thy right hand upholdeth me. - Psalm 63:1-8 KJV

Day 31

Passion

What am I living for? This is the question you must ask yourself. Once you discover the answer to this question, you can develop a plan to pursue your passion. A person with a passion knows exactly what they are called, appointed and anointed to do on this earth, and keeps the flame of passion burning with inspiration that will keep them motivated, rejuvenated and leaves little room to procrastinate.

First, setting short-term and long-term goals will help you to stay focused on building a positively awesome future.

Secondly, fulfilling your dreams and aspirations that will lead you toward greatness! Enhance your ability to accomplish your ambitions in excellence.

Thirdly, think about the choices you are making in your spiritual, personal and professional life. Consider two perspectives, whether they are positive or negative, right or wrong or good or evil. *The choice is yours.*

Fourthly, passionate people live their lives with a purpose, striving to get to the finish line in spite of adversity or tragedy. They keep treading the water, come what may.

Fifthly, people who live a life driven by purpose, fervently take baby steps to accomplish the easier task with the medium mission well in sight but ultimately endure until they cross the finish line. Any kind of set-back or obstacle is just another set up as passionate people are positive thinkers who don't panic at sudden calamity. They are creative thinkers, writers and optimistic people.

Sixthly, people who have no purpose in life are like a ship without a sail, like salt that's lost its savor or a burning lamp without its oil. When the bridegroom comes like a thief in the night, they are cast out because they had no plan to be ready for His unexpected return. Go-getters, positive thinkers and optimistic believers will spot a person without purpose a half a mile away.

Seventhly, when passion is what you live, love, laugh, breath, sleep, utter, imagine, believe and become, then the answer to the aforementioned question will be, my God-given purpose is to be of service to others and make their lives better by fulfilling that which I am called, appointed and anointed to do. In essence, you will be doing as God has commanded you: to serve your fellow man, always walking in agape, which is the greatest love of all.

Finally, keep the flame of passion burning bright.

Day 32

God's Presence Is Real – So Learn How To Listen To Him

Your presence is the most amazing thing I have ever experienced, Lord. There is nothing in this world that could ever compare to being in your presence, dear God. Your glory is such an overwhelming joy that I can't explain! It always floods my soul as my cup of love, hope and joy is running over with your glory in this vessel and body that my spirit resides in, Lord.

I can't even sing a song or hum a melody that will enlighten others under the power of your anointing unless your Spirit overtakes me with the power you have placed in me for your glory. All that I can express is that ever since I have experienced the glory of your goodness, and received a tiny glimpse of your presence, Lord – it is the ultimate high – higher than anything I have ever experienced in life, and I thank you for your love for me. I am fully aware and persuaded that you are real and that you are a God that speaks to your children.

Day 33

God Is With Me Right Now

God is with me right now
My eyes can't see Him
My hands can't touch Him
My nose can't smell Him
My ears can't even hear Him

God is with me right now
I know He is with me because the Bible tells me so
I know He is with me because my Mama and my Daddy
tell me so
I know He is with me because the preacher said He will
never leave me nor forsake me
I know He is with me always even until the end of my
life on earth

God is with me right now
Even when my world is crashing down like an earthquake
Even when my family and my friends turn their backs on me
Even when I have just two or three dollars in my pocket and a
zero-bank account balance
God is with me now because I can sense Him in the atmosphere

God is with me right now
Quietly I listen to hear His voice
Diligently I seek ye first His everlasting kingdom
Honestly, I pour out my heart that is bleeding for His love
Obediently I do whatever He tells me to because I know
He's real

God is with you right now
Just think about how everything has worked out for your good
God is with you right now; don't you know He loves you so much
God is with you right now but you must believe Him right now
God is with you right now but you must trust in Him only and depend on Him

God is with you right now
God is with me right now
God is with us through thick and thin and any kind of weather
God is with all of His children all over the world
God is with you right now

Day 34

Suicide Is Not An Option

Stop! Don't do it, because suicide is not the answer! No matter how hard life gets, don't give up! Don't quit! Jesus is the answer for the world today. I urge you, please give Jesus a try right now before you just end it all!

Life is worth living.

"Heaviness in the heart of man maketh it stoop: but a good word maketh it glad. The righteous is more excellent than his neighbour: but the way of the wicked seduceth them. The slothful man roasteth not that which he took in hunting: but the substance of a diligent man is precious. In the way of righteousness is life: and in the pathway thereof there is no death." - Proverbs 12:25-28

THINGS

Things Are About To Happen
Don't Lose Your Faith

Things Are About To Manifest
Don't Give Up Hope

Things Are About To Come To Pass
Don't Ever Stop Believing

Things Are About To Get Better
Don't Give Up On Your Future

Things Are Working Together For Your Good
Don't Forget That God Is In Control

Things Will Be Added Unto You
Don't You Know That You Deserve The Best?

Day 35

I Heard The Voice of God

When we pray, we are communicating to God from our own understanding.

When we meditate, God is talking to us so we must position our posture to hear God speak to us.

Living a disciplined life walking and praying in the Spirit, as often as you can, will enhance your ability to stay focused on the things of God, which is the most purposeful, positive and peaceful thing you could ever do for yourself.

Our mind must always be at peace, our body postured towards heaven, and our spirit always ready and willing to listen when the Holy Spirit is moving us to fulfill God's purpose in our lives.

REFLECTIONS

I pause to take a moment to reflect on the day that changed many of our lives in New York City, as well as America as we once knew it -- the day we call 9/11. God spoke to me twice that day in an audible voice. The first thing He said to me was, "Linda, go back into your apartment and read the 91st Psalm." I obeyed and did as the Lord instructed me to do – I reentered my apartment at exactly 7:10 am and read Psalm 91, not once, not twice, but three times. About 25 minutes later as I was driving my car on the New England Thruway going 95 South admiring what was the most beautiful day I had ever seen; my eyes were fixed on the New York City skyline. It was beautiful, and the Twin Towers are what stood out to me the most. I was driving pretty fast as I was running behind schedule, not understanding why

God had delayed me by asking me to go back into my apartment to read Psalm 91. I lived in New Rochelle, a 15-minute drive to the Bronx where I normally drove and parked my car daily at the Pelham Bay train station, the last stop on the number six train in the Bronx. There I heard God speak to me once again in an audible voice.

He said, "keep going!"

Both times the Lord spoke to me, it was a still, small voice. You know? The same still small voice that the prophet Elijah heard at Mt. Horeb; Abraham heard when God spoke to him and promised him a son and told him that he would be the father of many nations; the voice that the Apostle Paul heard on his road to Damascus, and the same still, small voice that Moses heard at Mt. Sinai.

There are so many profound moments of my life, especially the times when I have experienced hearing the voice of the Almighty God speak to me audibly, as well as the most sovereign acts of His kindness towards me, and the most amazing supernatural experiences that have brought me to the place I am at today in my walk as a born-again believer. It has activated my faith that keeps getting stronger and stronger in God. Although I have written many stories, the one on 9/11 is a true testimony of my faith in God and His miraculous power.

Day 36

Yesterday, Today and Tomorrow

I looked out my window early this morning as I glared out into the wintry mix and the darkened clouds were hiding the bright blue sky. The crystals were sparkling from the pure white snow that fell down from the clouds, all the way up in the sky above, reminding me that God is the perfect illustrator and the artist of my soul. He shapes me and molds me with His gentle, loving hands that press my spirit and make me what He wants me to be. My eyes were pleasantly amazed as I looked out into the horizon of God's firmament, amazed at the glorious sight of the snowflakes that fell down on the trees, limbs, branches, and the grassless lawn as the wind blew a sudden breeze that pierced my soul.

As I closed the window shed, I wanted to draw nearer to God and spend some quiet time alone with Him in fellowship. So, I began to pray, thanking Him for this brand-new day that He has made while I was rejoicing and being glad in that moment for a new day. I suddenly realized that today will be my only today, yesterday will be my latest memory of the things that transpired in my past, and tomorrow will be my only new hope for my future. So therefore, I will not worry about tomorrow and have no regrets for yesterday. I will live my life to the fullest today and be thankful to God that He chose me for this new day that He has made with me in mind.

Day 37

Quietness Is Essential To Hearing The Voice of God

For as long as I have been a Christian, it is at this very season and time of my life that I have come to the realization that communicating with God is more important than ever before. We are living in a time of uncertainty, when crime, murder and death is at an all-time high.

Earthquakes, wars and terrorism are more prevalent. We are living in a world full of wickedness and those who are in authority holding offices of the Presidential seat and the hierarchy positions have dishonored our country taking advantage of their power as leaders. It is shameful that instead of instilling Godly principles and enforcing the laws of our land for us to follow, they are doing the opposite and leaving our young people without role models to follow. Children are so unruly and disrespectful not only to their elders, teachers and their parents, but they are killing their parents and each other. Police shootings and brutality amongst minorities are also on the rise, and justice may never be done on earth, but in the courtroom of God, He will give us true justice and peace.

For the love of money, which is the root of all evil and the pursuit of greed has made many of lost souls succumb to the evil desires of their hearts. Whatever it is that has separated a people and a country that was built on the motto of righteous living, "In God We Trust," is quickly being done away with and quickly fading. We need to get back to the basics of that which our ancestors, who communicated with our God, and who still speaks to us today. Dr. King must be turning in his grave, ashamed of the racial injustices that still exist in this world today.

The question I want to leave you with is, "Are You Still Listening to God?" One of the ways you can hear Him speak to you is incorporating quietness and spending time alone with God. Quietness is essential to hearing the voice of God.

Day 38

You Don't Know My Story

One of the most important lessons in my life is how I have learned to meditate on God's Word and listen to Him. God has brought me through so many trials and tribulations, and today I can share my testimony of love, peace, joy and victory. Life and favor have found me, meeting me right smack in the middle of the most challenging times of my life. I once feared the dark because I was always being exposed to the things that no child should ever be exposed to. But, in the midst of it all, there is only one person who I can attribute my ability to write my story of how the favor of God upon my life has led, guided and protected me from fear and hurt. God also healed me from childhood trauma / sexual abuse and torture that crippled my confidence for always seeking approval from others in every area of my life. I can only attribute this to the God I serve, my Risen Lord and Savior, Jesus Christ who has healed me giving me a testimony. My testimony is my story, which allows me to be free as I am righteous now and justified by the blood that was shed of Jesus Christ.

I am delivered and want to jump up and down because of how excellent and wonderful God has been to me. I am so at peace and have so much joy, even when I am not happy about something or am faced with life challenges. You see, dear reader, I have come to a place where I realize that happiness and joy are not the same. The joy of the Lord is my strength, and joy is a true demonstration of my new found freedom and my life as an overcomer. I am an overcomer – fully equipped for the spiritual battle that is before me, daily. God has brought me out of the miry clay and placed my feet upon a rock to stay because the greater one, Jesus, lives inside of me and the power of the

Holy Spirit takes me higher in God. I ask God to endow me. The only thing I want in my life, more than having millions and billions of dollars, or the greatest thrill that comes from satisfying the flesh or traveling the world, is that of knowing Jesus in the power of His Resurrection. I want to operate and function under God's anointment of the Holy Spirit.

Day 39

The Vicissitudes of Life

When the vicissitudes of life have overpowered your life, the spirit of God will sustain you. When everything is upside down in your life, God is empowering you by His Spirit. Sometimes God will use an incident in your life to make an impact in the lives of others.

The Beatitudes is like the opposite of the vicissitudes of life. We should focus on what Jesus said every time He spoke to the multitudes saying,

"And seeing the multitudes, he went up into a mountain: and when he was set, his disciples came unto him: And he opened his mouth, and taught them, saying,
Blessed are the poor in spirit: for theirs is the kingdom of heaven.
Blessed are they that mourn: for they shall be comforted.
Blessed are the meek: for they shall inherit the earth.
Blessed are they which do hunger and thirst after righteousness: for they shall be filled.
Blessed are the merciful: for they shall obtain mercy.
Blessed are the pure in heart: for they shall see God.
Blessed are the peacemakers: for they shall be called the children of God.
Blessed are they which are persecuted for righteousness' sake: for theirs is the kingdom of heaven.
Blessed are ye, when men shall revile you, and persecute you, and shall say all manner of evil against you falsely, for my sake. Rejoice, and be exceeding glad: for great is your reward in heaven: for so persecuted they the prophets which were before you."- Matthew 5: 1-12

We must learn to listen obediently as we meditate and hear God speak. Listening prayerfully and submissively has been the most valuable lesson in my life. Hearing the voice of God has motivated me to do His will. Listening to God has changed my life in such a way that I desire nothing more than to listen to the God who made Heaven and earth, who has all power in His hands, who wants nothing more than a surrendered heart and mind that trusts Him completely.

Day 40

A New and Better Me

Self-love is something that every human being was created to do. Loving oneself is the beginning of living your life well, because in order to love others, you must first love yourself.

"Therefore, if anyone is in Christ, the new creation has come: The old has gone, the new is here!" - 2 Corinthians 5:17 (NIV)

Because of who God is in my life, I give Him all the glory, honor and the praise. I thank Him daily for all of the marvelous things that He has done for me. I worship the Lord in the beauty of His holiness. God is a good God... yes, He is and forever shall be my Savior.

A new and better me has become my newest discovery of myself today. I believe that God has made me to prosper in every area of my life. Embracing the natural person that I am has been the most rewarding part of my 40-day journal and an amazing journey to share with you.

In closing of my 40 Day Journal, *Positive Thinking Will Make You Happy – Mind, Body & Soul*, I pray that the blessings of God will overtake you like never before as you continue to seek Him while He may be found. Until my next journal, always remember that you are positively awesome!

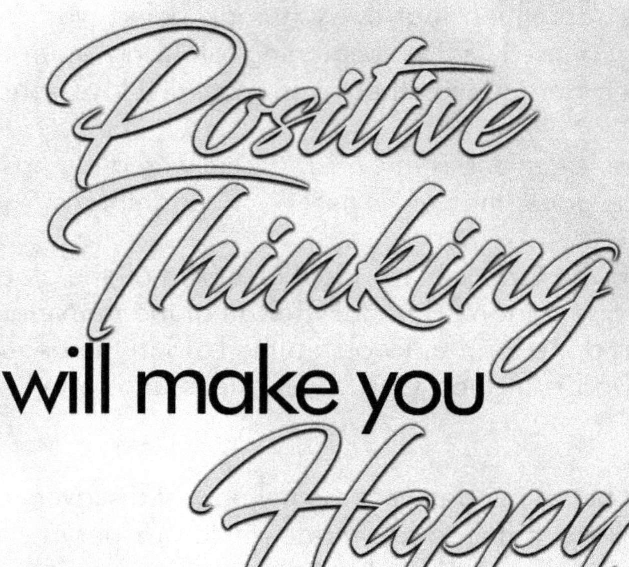

MIND, BODY, & SOUL

— ABOUT AUTHOR —

Meet the Author

LINDA M. JOHNSON

Linda Marshae' Johnson is the Senior Director of Artist & Repertoire for RJC Productions / Orchard SONY. Linda has been a talent scout for more than 20 years where she has organized and conducted auditions and talent searches for singers and actors for many directors, managers and producers in the New York Metropolitan area for various stage plays, concerts, commercials, movie shoots and more. Additionally, Linda is the Director of the Christian Drama Workshop and the Assistant Director of Titus Walker's Ujamaa Black Theater in New York City. Linda comes with a lot of talent, which stems from her involvement in the music industry as a recording artist and actress. She is a singer, actress, radio host, creative writer, producer, theater trainer, talent scout/life coach, author and motivational speaker. She currently holds a full-time position as a professional executive assistant of a major financial institution in New York City, where she has more than 30 years of experience.

Linda has been a member of many recording ensembles and gospel choirs throughout her career. She sang with the Late Pastor Clinton Utterbach & the Praisers, the United Pentecostal Choir (UPC), The A.K. Ensemble, Royalty, Another Great Blessing (AGB) Gospel Choir, Eternal Light Community Choir, and Ron Crichlow & RCE Gospel to name a few. In addition, Linda has worked with many producers as a test vocalist to prepare and arrange songs for other artists to sing and perform, as well as demo songs for various well-known artists with PokerFace Entertainment, Pelican Island Records, Troupe Records and Oleyoungin Productions. Linda currently works with many talented vocalists to get them signed on as recording artists with RJC Productions, as well as managing how they conduct themselves as professional gospel and inspirational artists.

Linda has hosted a call-in radio talk show called, "The Truth On The Positive Tip" with a holy hip-hop, all-female rap group "i4ni." She also has future plans start her own radio station for "The Truth On The Positive Tip" by spring 2020. She has been in many Broadway and Off-Broadway Productions with Titus Walker's Ujaama Black Theatre, playing the leading lady in "For the Love of My Black Woman," "The Gospel of the Harlem Renaissance," and "Please Don't Take My Rhythm & My Blues." She also appeared in El DeBarge and Kenneth "Baby Face" Edmond's video "Where Is My Love." Linda has also held extra roles in the soap operas "As the World Turns" and "All My Children."

Linda earned her Master of Fine Arts degree in creative writing with honors from the College of New Rochelle in 2019. She is a graduate of The Christian Bible Institute Seminary (CBIS) where she earned her associate degree in 2019, as well as her certificate in Biblical studies in 2015 – where she was named salutatorian of her graduating class. She also received her bachelor's degree in communications, with a minor in broadcast journalism, in 2002 from The College of New Rochelle, where she graduated with honors.

Linda is a co-author of the book, "Love Grounded by Grace," alongside Tenaria Drummond-Smith and is also working on her first book to be published in the summer of 2019. She is the daughter of author and evangelist Anne Gaynelle Johnson who wrote the book "Tear of a Man" and "Let The Healing Begin." Her mother has also produced her own CD and many stage plays that Linda has directed. Linda is a deaconess and married to Minister Thomas Wesley Johnson, IV, CFO of RJC Productions. She is the proud step-mother of five children and has six grandchildren. She and her husband currently attend church at the Powerhouse St. Luke C.O.G.I.C under the leadership of Pastor Sanford L. Henderson and Lady Sharon Henderson in the Bronx, New York.

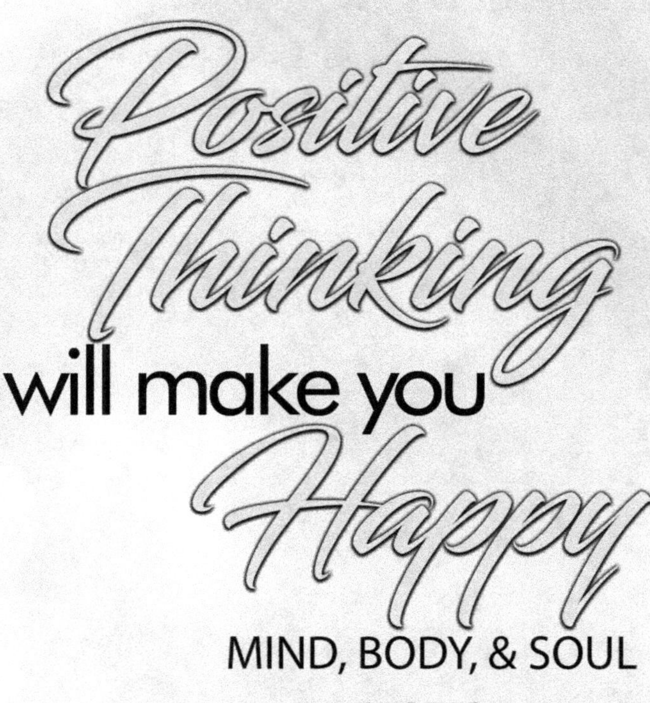
Positive
Thinking
will make you
Happy
MIND, BODY, & SOUL
— NOTES —

Rainbows

Every time I see a rainbow, it reminds me of God's covenant and promise to Noah to never cover or destroy the earth with water. The rainbow is our reminder of God's promise and sovereign love to all mankind.

This 40-day journey was well worth the sacrifice it took to inscribe every word of what resulted in this journal. The significance of the number 40 insinuates great importance of a new generation to commence a new thing as we are living in a world that is expeditiously evolving due to emerging technology. Today, we live in a "tech-savvy" world were the Millennials are shaping the future. Hopefully, they will never forget about our Risen Lord and Savior Jesus Christ who is the same yesterday, today, and forevermore.

If you have been inspired by the words in this journal, write your thoughts in the NOTE section.

NOTES

NOTES

NOTES

NOTES

NOTES

NOTES

NOTES

NOTES

NOTES

NOTES

NOTES

NOTES

NOTES

NOTES

NOTES

NOTES

NOTES

NOTES

NOTES

NOTES

NOTES

NOTES

NOTES

Also Available From Bestselling Author
LINDA M. JOHNSON

Linda M. Johnson Co-Author Books

Available at
amazon.com BARNES&NOBLE.com
www.bn.com

Also Coming Soon

Positive Thinking Will Make You Happy:
In The Valley of The Shadows (I heard the voice of God)

Violated Victim Validated Victor
A true story of my life as a sexually abused child who overcame childhood trauma through the Power of God and finding my way to living a victorious life as an adult

www.positivethinkingwillmakeyouhappy.com

 @thinkpositivelj   @positivethinkinglj  @lindajohnsonpo1

www.ingramcontent.com/pod-product-compliance
Lightning Source LLC
Chambersburg PA
CBHW070449170726
48291CB00005B/1674

* 9 7 8 1 9 4 2 8 7 1 6 8 2 *